The Beachiest Bits of
MAROONED ON THE MAINLAND™

Written and Drawn by J.B. Rafferty

www.jbrafferty.com

Book and Cover design by J.B. Rafferty

ISBN: 978-0-9966072-3-0
First Edition: December 2016

I even said, "Stop bothering the nice tiki man."

So I tell this tourist from New York, "Hey. if you really want a
tiki barber, I'll carve you a tiki barber."

Keep it up.   It's not too late to trade you in for a lizard.

Now that's what I call alcohol abuse.

Let's blow this tiki bar, he says. We can hide in that pumkin truck!

Tiki mugs? Why I just sold the lot of them to that nice young man.

The Beachcomber takes Buffét on his first snorkling adventure.
"Nice fishies! Nice fishies!"

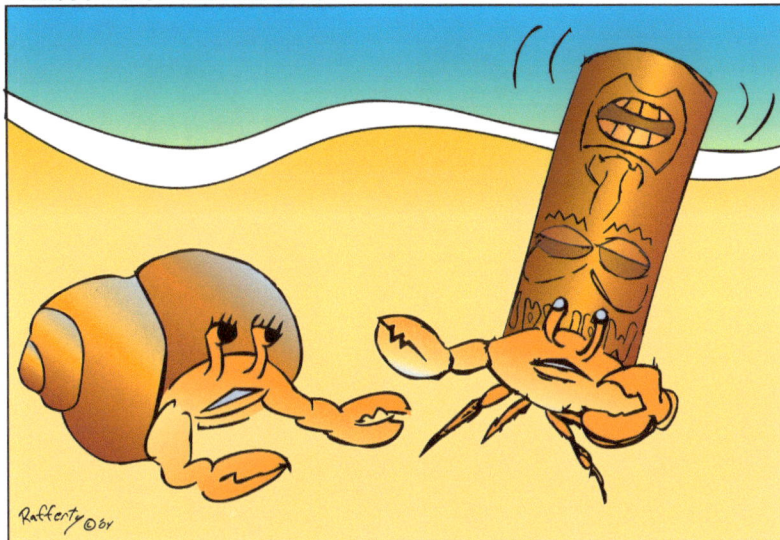

Oh no you don't. We're married now, and your wild bachelor pad
days are over.

Good parrot.

"Ouch, I think you missed a spot with that suntan lotion."

"Aye, yer a fancy boy.   Aren'tcha?"

Whoops Hon, must've swam out of my trunks.
Oh sure, run away! And they're not called tenticles!

Hey Man, I don't care if pee is the only way to soothe a jellyfish sting! You keep the heck away from me, and zip that thing back where it belongs!

Sand! Some crazy bastard built our castle out of sand!
We're all doomed!

Hey, dis aint beer! It's some kinda fruity sissy drink!

Sh-sh-sh-sh-shark!

Do you mind if I cut in?

Don't be silly, Silly, of course it's happy hour food.

Oh god, she's nuttier than a Monkey Flip, she's a cling-on,
and she just got me kicked out of my favorite tiki bar.
Please disregard my previous prayers to hookup with her.

MAROONED ON THE MAINLAND™

Hey sailor, why don't you lose the bimbo and meet me at the beach?

Bring it on, Biped!

MAROONED ON THE MAINLAND™

Strange, but I'm having second thoughts about dumping Fern. I didn't realize how hot she can be.

They are never going to believe this at TikiCentral.com.

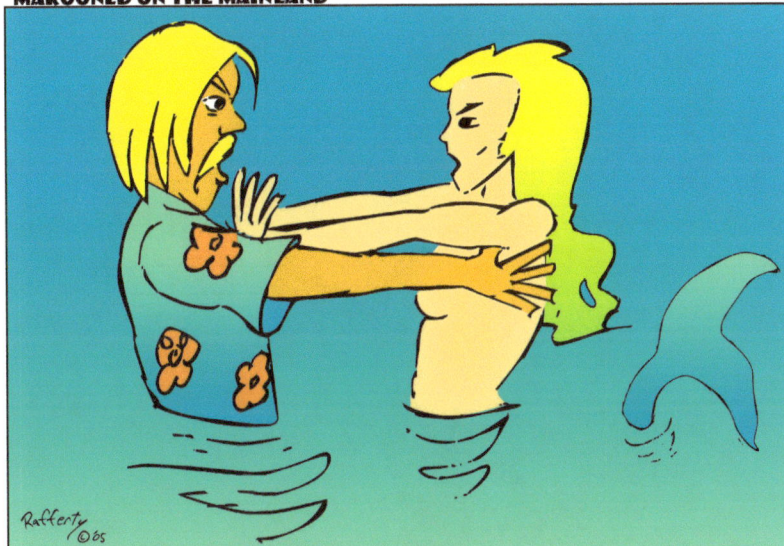

No Silly, first I spread my eggs on a coral bed, and then you...
wha...what were you thinking?!

A Missionary, a Headhunter, and a Zombie walk into a tiki bar.
The bartender says, "We don't serve Zombies here."
The missionary asks, "Do you serve Suffering Bastards?"

Thus began the infamous Babinga Beach Sno Cone fight of 2005.

The Beachcomber meets the Public Poolcomber.

Let me tell you the truth about swimmin' with bowlegged women.

I remember when people used to come to the beach and press shells against their ears.

Easy now, just a little pressure will open the toughest clam.

There's a shucker born every minute.

I think this guy is trying to mess with our heads.

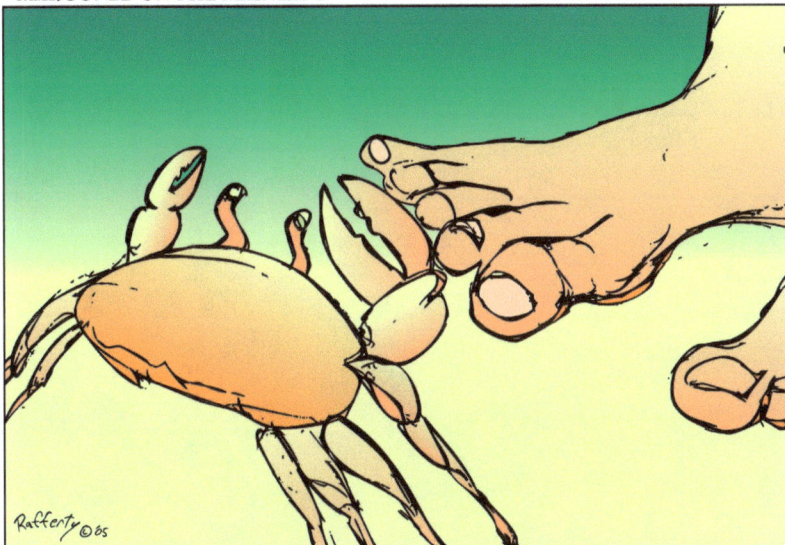

Eeny meeny miny moe, catch a tourist by the toe...

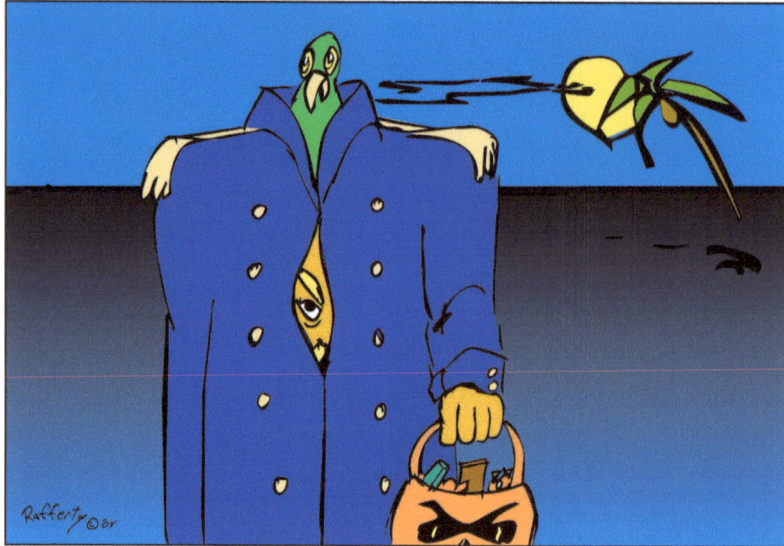

Trick or treat, smell my feet, give me a cracker,
or I'll crap on this guy's head.

It's funny how one corndog/bearclaw/cotton candy-eating sickie
can turn the Tilt-a-whirl into spin art.

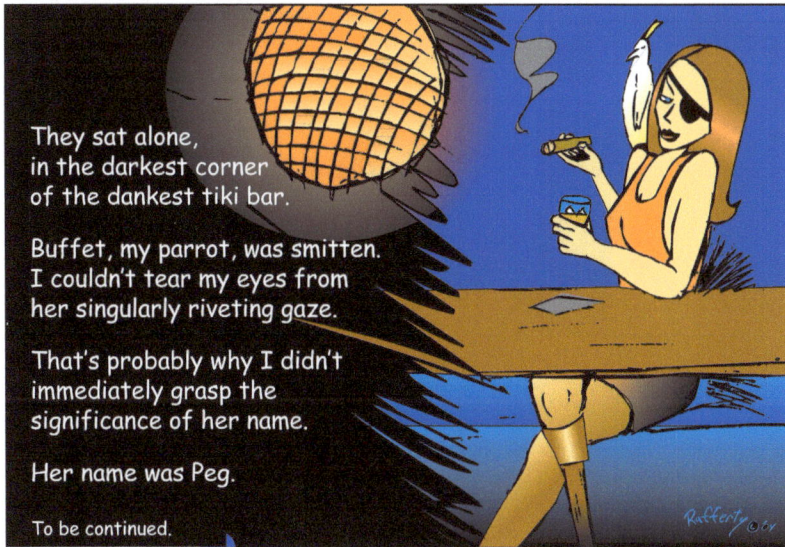

MAROONED ON THE MAINLAND™

They sat alone,
in the darkest corner
of the dankest tiki bar.

Buffet, my parrot, was smitten.
I couldn't tear my eyes from
her singularly riveting gaze.

That's probably why I didn't
immediately grasp the
significance of her name.

Her name was Peg.

To be continued.

MAROONED ON THE MAINLAND™

She was the epitome of style and
grace, except during our nightly
strolls on the beach.

Her peg leg kept sinking in the sand.
Right up to the hilt.

It was a housing boon for fiddler
crabs that summer.

To be continued...

MAROONED ON THE MAINLAND™

On our first date she brought me to a high-stakes poker game.
I knew I had Peg and the Captain beat. But the Zombie...
I just couldn't read him.

To be continued...

MAROONED ON THE MAINLAND™

Peg and the Captain folded.
I was sure the zombie would call.
He raised, with the keys to his hot rod.
I had no choice but to call, and put
Buffet onto the pot.

To be continued...

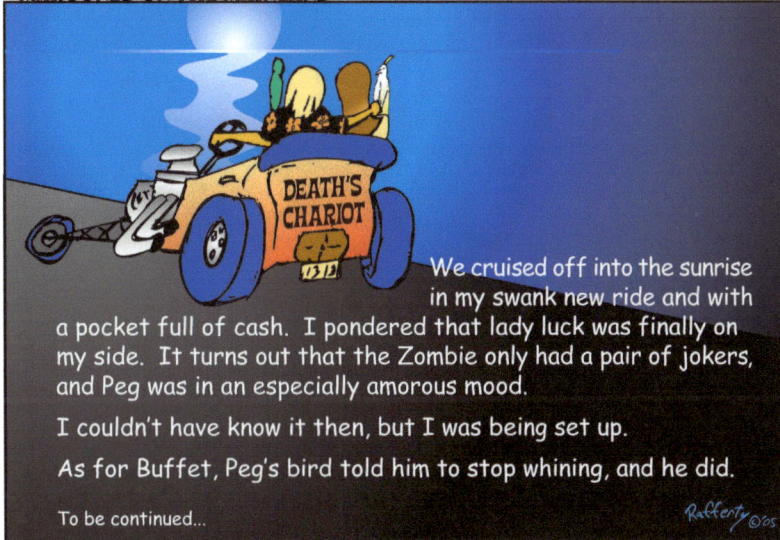

We cruised off into the sunrise in my swank new ride and with a pocket full of cash. I pondered that lady luck was finally on my side. It turns out that the Zombie only had a pair of jokers, and Peg was in an especially amorous mood.

I couldn't have know it then, but I was being set up.

As for Buffet, Peg's bird told him to stop whining, and he did.

To be continued...

Rafferty ©05

The morning after, Peg kicked back on a chaise lounge and nursed a couple Banana Daiquiris, while I showed my gratitude, I mean love, the best way I knew how.

I carved a tiki on her peg leg.

To be continued.

Rafferty ©05

Buffet and Peg's bird picked my favorite mystery bowl to nest in. In fact, he left a special present in every one of my tiki mugs.

He was holding a grudge because I bet him against the Zombie.

I decided to start my mug collection fresh, and sell these soiled ones on ebay.

To be continued.

Rafferty ©05

I kept telling the persistent voice on the other end that he had the wrong number. Peg overheard, and said that it must be for her.

"It" was going down tonight, outside the Motiki tiki soap factory.

And Peg had an alias. It was Ilene.

To be continued.

Rafferty ©05

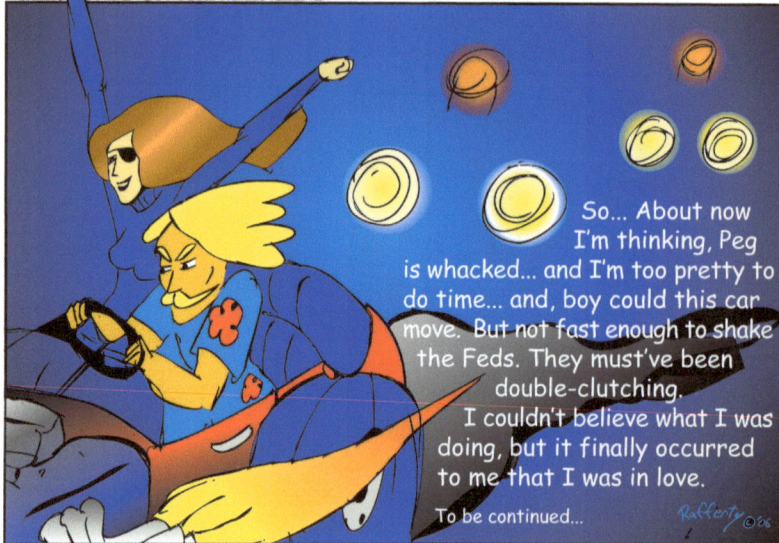

So... About now I'm thinking, Peg is whacked... and I'm too pretty to do time... and, boy could this car move. But not fast enough to shake the Feds. They must've been double-clutching.
I couldn't believe what I was doing, but it finally occurred to me that I was in love.

To be continued...

Rafferty ©06

We raced into a pea soup-like fog. Peg said to hang a right. I did. Dear lord, we were on a fishing pier.

We were corned like poi at a luau.

To be continued...

Rafferty ©06

Somehow, we landed in one piece on a ship. I was still hyperventilating as the Zombie checked out "his" hotrod for damage, the Cap'n did a quick inventory of his bootleg records, and Peg was telling me I would make a great pirate, and would love life in Bora Bora.

I was feeling trapped.
I don't wanna be a pirate.

To be continued...

I couldn't blame Buffet for deciding to leave with them. In the end, I just couldn't go. Peg was upset... livid even, and I would miss her...

... but it's not like I didn't have responsibilities back home.

To be continued.

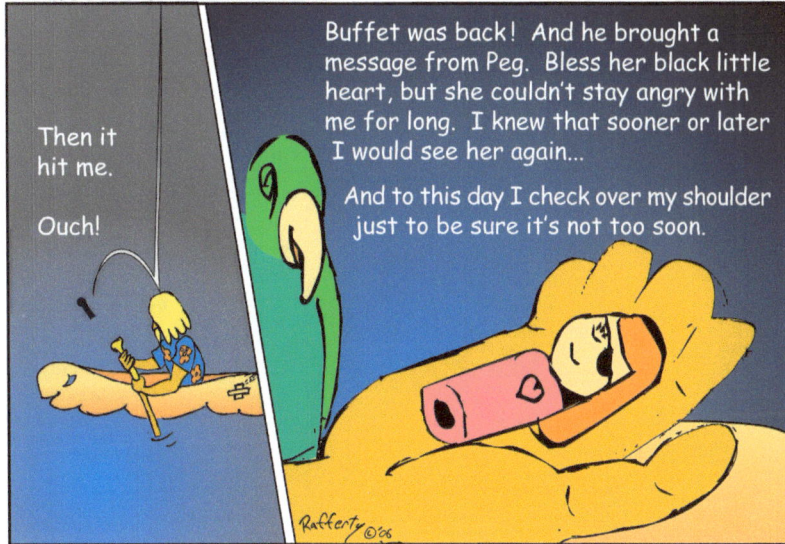

Then it hit me.

Ouch!

Buffet was back! And he brought a message from Peg. Bless her black little heart, but she couldn't stay angry with me for long. I knew that sooner or later I would see her again...

And to this day I check over my shoulder just to be sure it's not too soon.

Laidback New Yorker, my butt. Just wait until he realizes that there's pineapple on his pizza.

"Nice catch, nothing, this is the bait."

While we at the Mai Kai appreciate your patronage, we suspect
that you have been living here for three days... Please sir,
we found your bedroll in the garden.

Lucky for us, Cindy's mom likes to drink!

Easter, island-style.

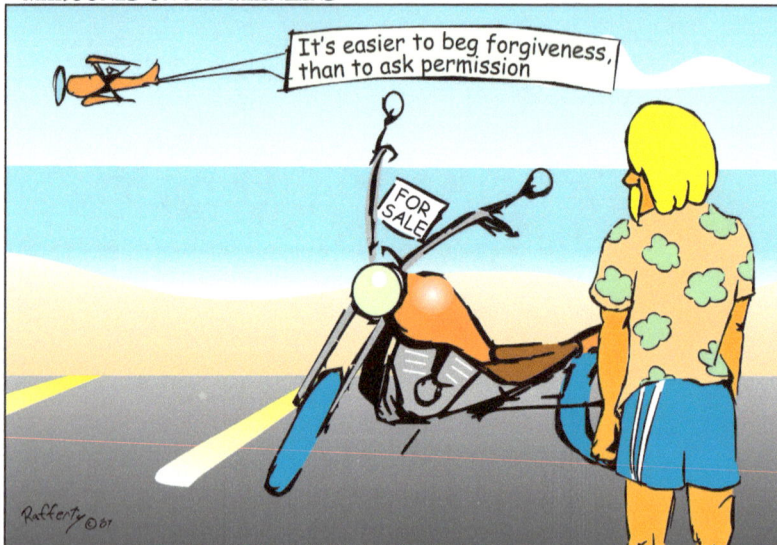

Hot enough for ya?

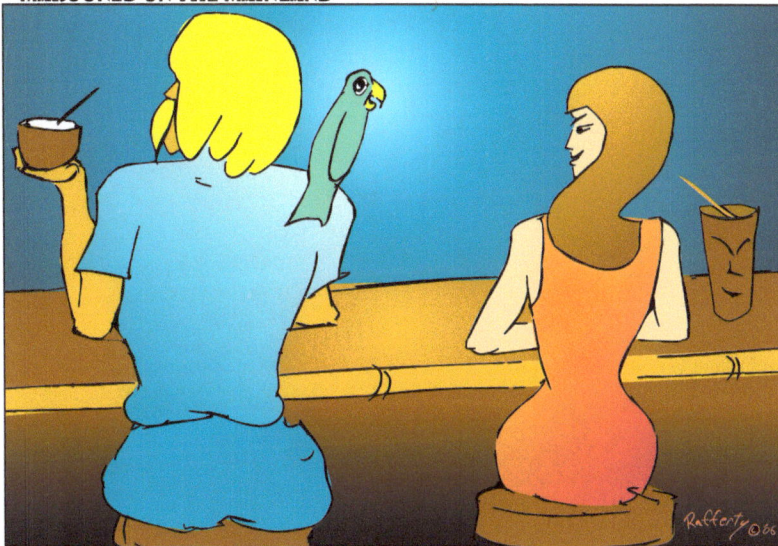

Hey, you're cute! You should check out my profile
on www.myspace.com/buff8.

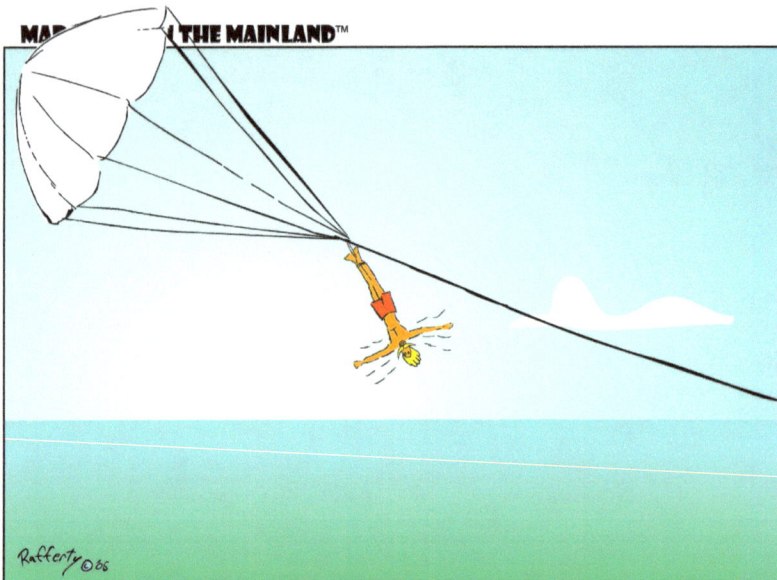

Never never never fall asleep on the beach after insulting the para-glide guys.

This guy is starting to freak me out!

I count two very happy Ellens, and one very terrified Jack.

Hey, there's a floaty in my drink!

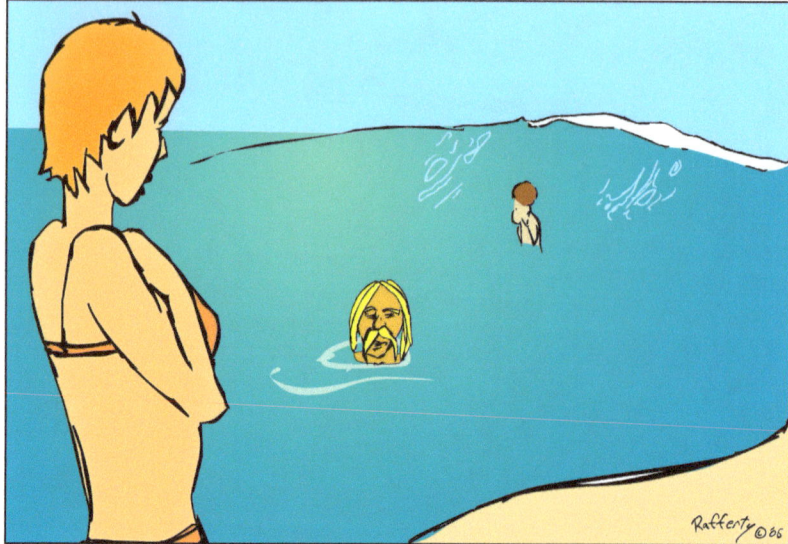

You don't have to worry about sharks! Just make sure there is always someone out deeper than you are.

Tom Cruise? He rented the bungalow just down the beach. You can't miss it.

It was clear from the start, that Carmine was not going to get along with the Slugmeyers.

The Beachcomber never naps past high tide.

Beach Ninja Dirty Trick #21
Create utter mayhem with a couple well-placed potato chips.

Please Don't Feed the Tikis

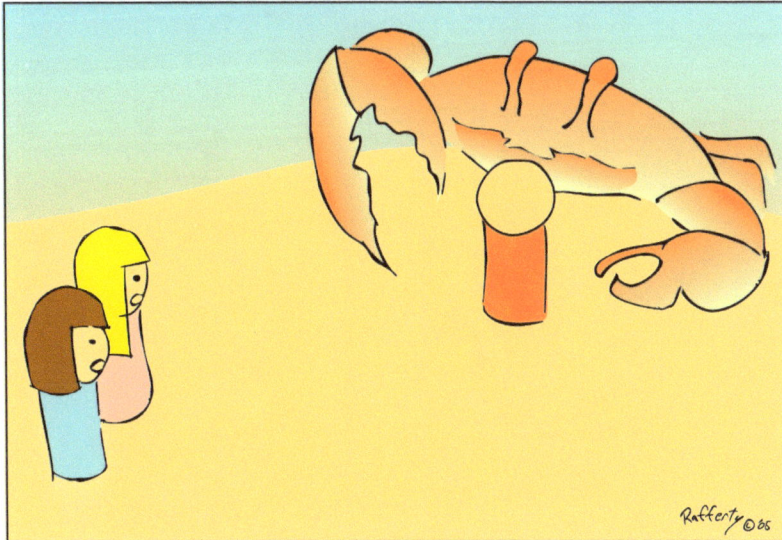

Run Billy run! Why is he just standing there?!

Most folks figure they've been in the water too long when their fingers turn pruny. The Beachcomber comes out when he gets barnacles.

That is the last time I laugh out loud when someone says that they
are a professional sand castle builder.

Hmmmn...perhaps I can slip out of this parachute, and fall back into the water before anyone looks up and realizes that my bathing suit has slipped down around my ankles.

You know, Buffet, one of these days, I too will have to face retirement.

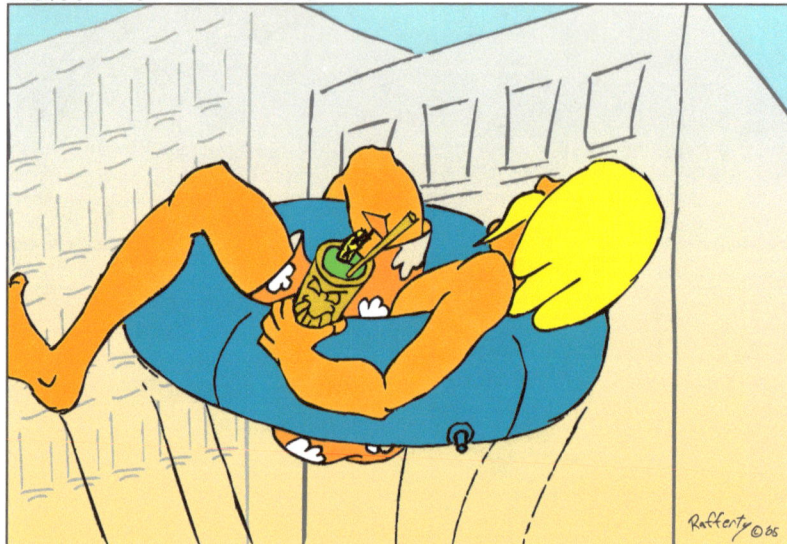

Here comes a balloon that is the new crowd favorite, as the wily Beachcomber moons the parade-goers all the way down Broadway.

He tells me, "The only way to be rebellious on New Year's Eve is to be fast asleep before midnight." I said I'd join the rebellion some year when I don't have a date either.

The Sweenys are starting to piss me off.

Hey Mon, you got something on your face...
no no a little to your left.

Fifty years of waking up, only to stare at that stupid grin.
I'm sick of it I tell you. Sick of it!

And a fine Happy St. Paddy's Day to yourself!

Not a chance Romeo! Not unless we find someplace where
my father won't walk in on us.

MAROONED ON THE MAINLAND™

It was an odd commission for a strange carving. The money was good, but I already spent it, and I promised to have it finished by tomorrow. Now I was racing against the approaching storm to meet my deadline.

I never met the woman who commissioned this carving, in fact I only dealt with her gorillas. As I watched it take a direct hit, I considered that she might not be the sort who tolerated excuses.

The next morning I faced my worst fear! There was nothing but a charred spot where "The Headhunter" once stood. It was my own darn fault for working so much mojo into this carving. Buffet said it best, "We have a runner!"

I would have to track down my own creation before it hurt someone. As I dusted off the telescopic sight on my semiautomatic blow gun with darts dipped in mojo-inhibiting serum, I wondered if my carving-come-to-life would view me as its father or as its god.

Exhausted after a fruitless day of tracking my creation, I stopped for a Mai Tai to clear my head. It was then that Buffet spotted the Headhunter in the mirror's reflection. My god, it was sneaking up on Paris Hilton!

Thwum

I had a clear shot at the Headhunter until the crowd jumped up to boogie to the new Crazed Mugs' tune. This would be the toughest shot of my life, but I had no choice. I waited for an opening and let fly one dart dipped in mojo-inhibiting serum!

To be continued...

MAROONED ON THE MAINLAND™

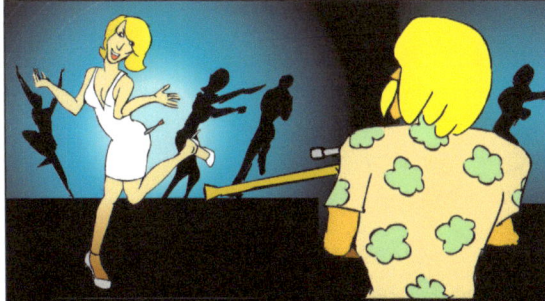

I missed my target, but all hell broke loose when Nicole Ritchie lost her mojo. I couldn't see Paris Hilton or the Headhunter in the ensuing stampede, and when the dust settled they were both gone.

Buffet took flight and spotted the Headhunter, with Miss Hilton, heading straight for the Hilton Hotel. My God, he must be taking her to Trader Vics to perform a virgin sacrifice.

I burst into Trader Vic's, ready for anything, except for this! The Headhunter, Miss Hilton, and uh, one of my mysterious benefactor's, uh... gorillas. They all looked dangerous and angry as hell. I didn't know which to shoot first.

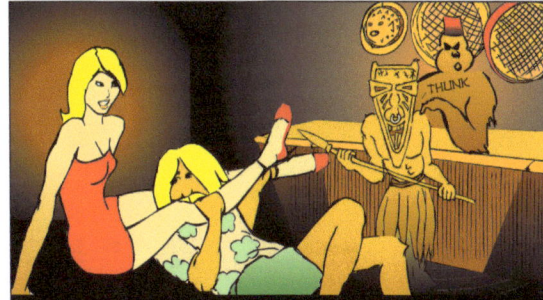

The next thing I know, I'm on the floor, and Paris Hilton has me in a Malaysian death-grip scissor hold. Then she struck the hardest blow of all. She said, "You deluded mess of a tikimon, the Headhunter never was alive."

It turns out the gorilla came early to collect the Headhunter. I don't know if I was relieved or disappointed that my creation had never come to life. I left without looking back, but often wonder if maybe I should have.   **The End**

We hope you enjoyed our twisted little tale of deception and intrigue, but remember, no actual mojo was lost and/or destroyed in the making of this comic.

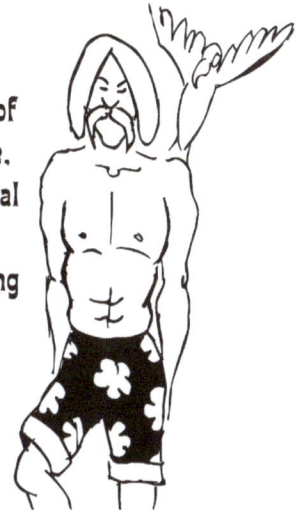

Tiki Tourist Trap.

www.ingramcontent.com/pod-product-compliance
Lightning Source LLC
Chambersburg PA
CBHW041545040426

42447CB00002B/53